BOOK BENCHERS
PUBLICATIONS
PRESENTS

THE REJECTIONS

Compiled By

Jeflin J.S

AELAY PUBLICATION

A dream come true for every writers out there. We spot every possible problem for the writers, help in rectifying them and guide them towards the best outcome. We make sure to understand your needs, dreams and expectations, and nourish them with our services and stop not until we fulfill your dreams. The writers have a right and freedom to choose what they want here. They have us to guide them through the hardest path until the end. Believe in us.

Aelay Publication - by a writer for the writers.

BOOK BENCHERS

Book Benchers is the affiliate of Aelay publication. Both the publication is handled by Astro.
Aelay plays the role of publishing solo books. And Book Benchers is epically for publishing anthologies.

Book Benchers have 2 different teams.
1. Tamil

2. English/Hindi

Never mind what our main motive is to help all the budding writers, who are seeking for their dream of publishing their own book to come true.

We are there to help out everyone.
In guiding for starting up with your carrier in compiling until finishing up your full book.

<u>COPYRIGHT</u>

First Edition: October 2021

Design And Executed by

 aelay Publish.com

ISBN : 978-93-5533-169-4
Page : 118
Price: Rs.220/-

ACKNOWLEDGEMENT

To list who all have helped us is difficult because they are so numerous and the depth is so enormous. We would like to acknowledge the following as being idealistic channels and fresh dimensions in the completion of this book.

We take this opportunity to thank the Co-authors for being a part of this book and submitting their beautiful writer-ups and making this book more special.

We would like to thank the publication team for providing the necessary facilities required for the completion of this book. We take this opportunity to thank our book editor for the moral support and guidance.

Lastly, We would like to thank every person who directly or indirectly helped me in the completion of the book especially my parents and peers who supported me throughout my book.

DISCLAIMER

This Anthology is a work of fiction. Our editors have tried their best to avoid any sort of plagiarism and the proof-readers have done their job of proofreading best on their part to expertise the book with unplagiarized and original content. Still if any appropriation detected, the editorial team is no where responsible, the author is solely responsible for such acts. We have well guided our co-authors to submit their original write-ups.

<u>FOUNDER</u>

IRUDAGA ASTRO

Irudaga Astro, From Tirunelveli, Founder of
Aelay and BB (Book Benchers)
He had completed his BE.
He has written 3 Tamil poetry book's which hits
the top list on social media!
His main aim is to allow the writers to publish
their words as their book rather than just Posting
them on Insta.

LINK AND POSTER MAKER

CATHERINE ASMI T

Catherine Asmi T, From Tirunelveli
She has completed her M.com
Her passion is Drawing and Designing.

TEAM HEAD

She is a passionate writer from Chennai. Writing makes her pressure go away. She had played the role of co-author for more than 100+ Antho's.
She would like to thank her parents and her Loveable Brother for supporting her rather than stopping her from what she wanted to do! For being the main reason for achieving her dreams. As well as for standing beside her in all the ups and downs.
Whenever she feels like she needs to get out of her stressful timing or feels like she needs peacefulness, she starts to paint, she would never mind sitting in the same place for so many hours when it comes to her painting. She believes that anyone could hurt her, But never her books could!!

Catch her in Insta and FB
Insta: @theinnocentheart
FB: KA. PARINASRI

INDEX

COMPILER

Jeflin J.S

CO-AUTHORS

1. Catherine Sheenna
2. Ahalya Merin. A
3. Yogesh Gurjar Chinu
4. Athira. A
5. Tahreem Afzal
6. Supriyacsk
7. Ankita Sarkar
8. S. Suganthi
9. Lispa Dabhi
10. Priya Singh
11. FareehaFaiyyaz
12. Samyuktha. S
13. Md. JunaidMondal
14. Manasvi Singh
15. Roger Ben .F
16. Bibhusmita Singh Samanta
17. F. Senita
18. Sananshika Malik
19. Rozy Paul
20. Naveen Bhardwaj
21. SrishtiMorya
22. SwayamshreeChakravarty
23. AnkitaNahar

24. Ananya P Mishra
25. DeeshaSoni
26. Berdhisha. P
27. Nilanjasha Howlader
28. Mohammed Niyaz
29. Sapna. P
30. Nabishbha S.S
31. Mansha Goyal
32. Dhanesh Ghanashyam Gawde
33. Anishka Nayak
34. Bashi Butt
35. Bidisha Bhattacharyya
36. Prachi Gupta
37. Neha Kumari
38. Soniya Varghese
39. Priya Das
40. Sushra
41. Srija Sadhukhan
42. Bandita Nahak
43. Sowndarya Harini Sampath
44. N.Krishnaveni
45. Smita G Naidu
46. Tejasvi Dev
47. Anns Fetrica
48. S.A. Alice Fatima
49. Cyilrisha A.M.
50. Kancharla Sai Sandeep

COMPILER

JEFLIN J.S

Her name is Jeflin. She is a budding writer. Currently, she is pursuing her bachelor's degree. She has decided to express her creative imaginations via short stories, poems and quotes. She is the co-author of many anthologies. This is her first book as a compiler.

IG : jeflin_14

REFLECTION OF REJECTION!

That was the moment looks like ending,

Her eye full of tears extending,

Her heart just hatred with blue,

She didn't even get a clue,

With head full of chaos, she stepped forward,

That was the time she under goes awkward,

She struck herself alone in the dark room,

Just like the room her future sight like gloom,

She just out viewed about her exclusion,

She just worked hard through intrusion,

She found her way through her aggression,

It led her to alter her rejection!

-JEFLIN J.S

CO-AUTHORS' DESK

SHEENA CATHERINE

Sheena Catherine is a girl with plenty of dreams. She is a nineteen years old girl who is still trying to achieve her dreams. Her pen is Sheenacathrinebelle. She likes to write poems, short stories, quotes etc. She is a broad-minded person. She believes that words speak greater than action so she writers from heart.

IG : sheenacathrinebelle

WHAT HURTS US MOST

The feeling that we don`t get back the love we give to others.

Expectations hurt.

The feelings of being rejected by one we loved.

Expectations hurt.

The feelings of being left alone by everyone at last.

Expectations hurt.

The feeling of being betrayed by our trusted ones.

Expectations hurt.

But still our minds wanting more, That`s what human nature.

It`s okay to get hurt,

Cuz we learn not to get hurt from the same thing again.

It`s okay to get hurt,

Cuz we learnt an important lesson from that pain.

It`s okay to get hurt,

Cuz it shapes us into a beautiful sculpture.

It`s okay to cry,

Cuz every single tear has its own way of healing.

Expectations hurt.

                              -CATHERINE SHEENA (Sheena Jane)

AHALYA MERIN

She is Ahalya, an Aesthete. She is an artistic writer who pens down her thoughts, dreams and dreams and desires vividly capturing petite details of details of daily life. She has a dashing personality, which enables her to spread hope and positivity through her fine stream of euphonious phrases. A tender soul who spending time with her cherished circles.

IG :ms_metero_shower_

SAD AND HAPPY

When joy and sorrow pedal,

You can reach a perfect level.

They are just letter,

Which can`t always header.

You are living as rental,

Both can be essential.

When you fall as judgmental,

They make you strong as parental.

With dejection, Dandelion can be blown,

But it can wakes up with its clone.

When failures enters,

Don't make yourself surrender.

Neither sad nor joy ever last,

Unless you make it equally biased.

Both moon and sun,

Can`t lead their life without a spun.

They are different with hot and cold,

But always make life composed.

It can be winter or spring,

Both can make you fly as wing.

-AHALYA MERIN .A (Ahalya)

YOGESH GURJAR CHINU

Her name is YogeshGurjar and nickname is Chinu, she is from Gautam Buddha Nagar district of Uttar Pradesh. She loves to write and read thoughts, has written more than 1300 poems and quotes. She has written as a co-author in 400 Anthologies. Her first solo book is titled (सच्चीबातें "चीनू").

IG : @yogeshgurjar369

LEARNING OF EXPERIENCE

That experience teaches,

It is not the text of a book,

Experience doesn`t come with age

Comes from facing the circumstance,

If you don`t make your dreams come true,

So someone else will hire you for himself,

Success comes from experience and

Experience always comes from bad experience,

Be it good or bad, one gets to learn from it,

It is experience that makes us understand the meaning of
every word,

Happiness is such a feeling,

What everyone is looking for

Grief is such an experience,

that everyone has,

Experience makes one feel grown up at a young age,

Experience teaches the most important lesson of life....!!

-YOGESH GURJAR CHINU

ATHIRA. A

Co-author Athira. A is a young poetess from Ernakulam, Kerala State. She has completed her Bachelors in Science stream from St. Teresa's College, Ernakulam. She has been writing poems for 15 years as her passions. Book reading and reviewing is also her major hobby.

IG : _athira_a_

EMAIL ID : athiraorminnu@gmail.com

WORDS LEFT UNTOLD

These words left untold
Are picking my heart;
And I am standing here;
All alone and dejected,
With these rheumy eyes,
With these shivering lips.

But this heart still hopes,
Those days will be back,
When you will treasure me
More than your own self;
And I will cherish you
More than you my own self.

My dear! Look at me again,
And let me to be with you;
Let the amorous gaze of you

Keep beating my heart again,
Let the sultry smile of you
Keep making me shy again.

-ATHIRA. A

TAHREEM AFZAL

She has done her Mathematics. Besides being a dream hunter, she is the girl who is traveling ion the path called 'life'. She doesn't complain for the obstacles, she just makes sure that her faith never gets blurry, as this is the only candle of light which keeps her going in dark night.

IG : reemsays789

THE REGRETFUL TEARS

Through these tears,

I shed those screams which are caged

behind my stitched lips.

This is my way

of speaking of my pain.

The pain that has its roots

in some unwanted miseries

that were set by no one else,

but by the persons

whom I made my world

This is my way to tell you that

I had lived a lie, considering myself the queen.

With myself now,

I am living a torturous truth,

believing that I was rejected and ignored

for the sake of some temporary glitters.

-TAHREEM AFZAL

SUPRIYA C.S.K

As a Co-author Supriya is a good writer from Chennai. She has completed her graduation in commerce stream. She has been writing poetry for more than 6 months as her passions. She wants to be an aspiring author in future.

IG :aridonoshikifuka

❖ Rejection doesn`t judge you,

  the ability is not a maestro

  believe yourself so can you

  achieve and prove one day.

❖ "Do not aim to accomplish

  anything in your first attempt of

  learning just think whether

  satisfying your heart's desire"

❖ "It is that success is not

  final and failure is not fatal for

  anybody in their life"

-SUPRIYA C.S.K.

ANKITA SARKAR

Ankita Sakar is a girl from Jamshedpur. She did her graduation on Hospitality Management and now majoring in child psychology. She has published her own book and has been a part of 7 anthology books. She has expressed her feelings through words.

IG: ankitasarkar_4

LIFE

No one knows better than yourself

So, stop listening to others,

About choosing the favorable paths,

Because if you fail,

No one will be on your side,

But it you succeed,

Everyone will be on your side,

This is called Trend.

Life is short either make it or break it,

But don`t waste it,

It blooms when you take care with love.

-ANKITA SARKAR

S. SUGANTHI

Suganthi has been writhing for over two years. She provides philosophical writings. Her educational background in English literature has given her a broad base for writings. Her books are available in amazon, kindle named Heartly Sayings and Healing journey-1.

IG : study.bucket

PAIN

Pain changes like season,

It changes every season

We get different pain in every month.

Life is a lesson in that pain is problem

One pain heals another pain come

This is life. Without problem

No one can live, everyone

Has a problem in life.

Heal the pain before we get

Another problem.

-S. SUGANTHI (chum_moon)

LIPSA DABHI

She is LipsaDabhi. She is an author and also a good co-author. She is eighteen years old; she is student of the computer engineering. She is extraordinary person. She is always a good leader. Her mam MrunalPrajapati is her inspiration person and also her motivator, her friend ChetnaRaval also supported to her and her mom Manisha ben and her father Nileshbhai also supported to her for any type of her creativity. She also wrote poems, short stories, shayries. Her creative collections are always best.

IG : _lipsa_dabhi_0829

❖ Failures is the one type of way of life,

   Don`t be panic for failures,

   We all are ready with new failures,

   So, don`t be afraid and stay with success.

❖ Sometimes rejections are better than acceptance,

   Rejections are part of life,

   Some rejections good for us,

   Rejections is one way of life.

❖ Struggles are way of your success,

   So, friendship with struggles so you never lose everything,

   You won everything with struggles,

   Stay with struggles and happy with struggles.

❖ Life lessons mean life part,

   Life is up-down and good-bad but,

    Always life is with us,

   Don`t be panic all life lessons is the part of life.

-LIPSA DABHAI (Desire)

PRIYA SINGH

Priya Singh is born & brought up in Dewas, MadhyaPradesh. She's a Proud daughter of her Father B.N.Singh (T.I.).She's completed Masters of Computer Science. She is a Former Educationist, Communication Trainer & Avid Reader. She's the Co-Author of the Anthologies:-"It's all about two phase : love & hate" ,"Words From Heart", "Fierce, Fearless N Flawed" & "In the way of borehole", "Unseen Blessings & "Sublime Love", "Mere Papa". All are available in Amazon. Till today, she's worked in 200+ Anthologies as a Co-Author & compiling 3. Her writing keeps her at ease. She mostly writes quotes on thoughts. She loves inspiring young minds.

IG :Instant__thoughts_

❖ Let it give you pain hurt let it, let it make you stronger than

    the way you were before, every hurt, every pain makes

    you stronger enough to deal with any kinda chaos life

    throws on you, stay strong, enjoy life being you.

❖ Life seems like a leaf,

    valued till stuck on branch of trees

    else unworthy as crushed below feets.

❖ We create our own monsters by our imaginations,

    We even create which doesn't exist,

    Whatever we are imagining, somewhere taking its form,

    So think before what you're going to imagine.

-PRIYA SINGH

FAREEHA FAIYYAZ

FareehaFaiyyaz is a student and a writer who is deeply intrigued by the universe of emotions and feelings. Her writeups are reflection of her journey of self-love. She is also co-published author who took part in more than 45+ anthologies.

IG :charmingfrequencie

LETTER TO SELF

Why failures bring me down?

I don`t know why success of others

Brings me down

Why is that thousands of times after,

I still hear we all aren`t equal

Why do I feel shattered still?

We might not be equal and same

Yet we are equal

But our difference are glitters of spectrum

We all bloom at our paces

Diving into oceans of self

And crafting through mundane charm.

-FAREEHA FAIYYAZ (Charmingfrequencies)

SAMYUKTHA. S

Samyuktha.S is a 16 years old aspiring writer and a compiler who loves to explore and learn. She has been writing for more than 3 years and has published a few of her works.

IG : 3xclusivedreamer_art

NEW BEGINNING

As the new year bells ring
At that late night hour
I stare at wooden door
And listen to that sound
As I play my memories
Of the same day
But from the previous year.

All I could remember
Was me crying
And talking to myself
Wishing for the best
All alone in a dim room
With little or no light

As I played my memories
Of the mountains I had to cross
I chuckled and said

"That was hard.
It doesn`t matter since it`s in the past"
While I tasted
The sweetness of success.

-SAMYUKTHA. S

MD. JUNAID MONDAL

Md. JunaidMondal is born and brought up in Kolkata. He is a student of standard 12. As it is a universal truth that poetry is the finer spirit of all living science. He believes that words have the power to transform the lives specially when they are used with poetic sensibility. He had penned his first poem entitled "Mom and Dad" at the age of 14. Since then, a sort of reality stamps deeply on his mind what Wordsworth said "poetry is the spontaneous overflow of mind" and indeed words came so gracefully and effortlessly that a book in 2019 "Read to Explore" published containing almost 50 poems.

IG: mjm03_offical

WALKING ALONE

I am out on a lonely road,

Feeling broken at times and sometimes get slowed.

But my target is locked now nothing can stop,

Let's chase down the greatness and reach the top.

My wings had a few scars which I got in my past,

But my faith helped me to recover fast.

All the time inside me goes a quest,

Which increases my hunger which I truly possess?

Throughout my journey I have been flying alone,

Thankful to those who cheated me and gone.

All my accompany you chaws,

But it may me stronger than I was.

I dedicate all the progress I made,

To my parents and a few well- wishers who never fade.

I know the fight has just started,

And not again for help, I will bleat.

-MD.JUNAID MONDAL

MANASVI SINGH

My name is Manasvi, I'm 14 years old and currently a high school student, I have a huge interest in arts whether it is poetry, fine arts or musical arts. I create art-related content on YouTube and Instagram (ManasviS. Art) in hopes of others finding their creative side and making people see this world isn't just black and white but is filled with amazing colors no one want to miss seeing & reminiscing.

IG : @thoughts_of_an_ecceentric_mind

HAND IN HAND

The rejections may look pretty easy or way too hard.
But it's only you who realizes, what they actually are.
It's only you who feels like, someone can actually have it all.
It's only you who tries, to vouch for all the pain and the loss.

Do I have to face all of them? Yes, I do.
Will it be worth it? I don't know.
These are the questions I ask her every day,
 and we are only left with a single sentence in consolation.

You want to be okay so, you will be okay.
After all, you gave your everything, even when these
 lights blind you constantly & consistently.
You always find a way to escape to the end of the tunnel.

So, we'll be here, Hand in hand, facing every rejection
that life has yet to give.

Maybe you'll leave my hand, maybe we'll smile,

maybe we'll glide through the pool of life with many grudges
and rough edges.

But isn't it the uncertainty that brings me all the joy?
 That makes me want to go far?
I guess it is, but you and I will keep figuring it out.
But we'll face them together forever.

- MANASVI. S

ROGER BEN. F

F. Roger Ben, is a budding poet & a young writer. He is pursuing Bachelor of science degree in Nursing, at RVS College of Nursing, Coimbatore. He resides in small village Annamangalam, near Perambalur district of Tamil Nadu. He has a vivid interest in writing poems, articles, quotes and short stories in English. His poems are treasured in insta and fb id" @ ParamindPoemVlogs". He has also played his role as Co - author in about 10 Anthologies. His dream is to do Doctoral fellowship in Pediatric Nursing.

IG : roger_ben_05

FAILURES :(:(:

Undergoing several failures,

I won`t put myself down,

And with my spirit high,

I will build the stairs,

And keep on moving forward,

With hard work and determination,

I will be stepping towards success.

Like a seed sown in the soil,

With the roots of hope deeper,

Diligently thriving the branches,

I will bloom into flowers and fruits,

In the garden of my victory...

-F. ROGER BEN

BIBHUSMITA SINGH SAMANTA

Writer Bibhusmita Singh Samanta writes motivational quotes, shayris, small poems on love, friendship etc. She believes that, sometimes rejections are required to make people realize what they actually deserve. Rejections make us bold, strong from both heart and mind. They teach us many things which even acceptance can't teach. So, take the rejections positively and correct yourself to make the best version of yourself.

IG :royal_princess_bibhusmita

REJECTIONS

Rejections are like poisoned arrows
Going straight into your heart.
Each hurtful word or cold silence
Break off a piece your tender loving heart
It takes away your self-belief,

It takes away your self-worth.
Each arrow of rejections tearing,
Until there`s little of self-worth
To fight these demons that are tearing you apart.

They show no mercy as they see you crumble,
They laugh at your demise.
They feed off your self-loathing
Like vultures until every piece of self-esteem has gone before
your very eyes.

But like the phoenix from the ashes, we will rise again!!
We will take their poisoned arrows and fire them back at
them!!
Every insult, every put-down will be thrown their way,
Until we rise up in triumph and fly away.

-BIBHUSMITA SINGH SAMANTA(@dil_ki_batein)

SENITA .F

Her name is Senita. F, she is facing her failures from her childhood and wants to build her own empire of success to stand infront of her rejections. She is just a simple girl who aches for a humble award.

IG : @iam_senita

❖ After Rejections, life becomes a marathon.

❖ Success seeks you, when rejection gives you another lesson.

❖ Rejections is not just falling down, but in standing up and facing it differently.

❖ Rejection is not just a word, but a feeling longing for success.

❖ Trust your handwork, though you reject for such peoples will be celebrated.

❖ Trying hard and getting rejected is not so bad than staying where you are defeated.

❖ New innovative ideas, makes you creative and defeats rejection.

❖ Never look at the rejected person as a failure for they holds the stone to achieve.

❖The feeling of rejection is unexplainable.

❖ Rejection happens to make your hard work more successful.

-F. SENITA (Anne)

SANANSHIKA MALIK

Sananshika Malik is an Indian writer author and founder of _the_stunning_ compiler_ company. She has started her writing career at the age of 19. She has completed over 40+ book at the age of just 19 and got a national record Holder by Anand Shree Organization too. She has also very much talented in Anchoring filed and has gained a lot medals in this field too. Her first book is Pita (A love of father) where she has described a father and a daughter love in a very beautiful way. Her most famous book are also mentioned there such as Pita (a love of father) Shh!! My fantasy world Chuddy buddy. Words of heart part 1 and 2 and many more like that.

IG :maliksanabshika_

LEARN FROM YOUR OWN REJECTIONS

Dia was in 16 when she fallen for someone at the age of teen she started thinking of marriage with that person. The boy and Dia was in same school but in different grade after getting talk they start dating with each other but later the boy has dumped her because Dia was not comfortable to give the boy what he wanted. And on that time Dia faced her Rejection for the first time in her life. She was totally breaking after all that was her first rejection and her breakup too. She went to the depression so badly and unfortunately on that time she did not had support of her family too. She started crying every time. And her health problem increased day by day. Dia was an emotional girl no one understands her easily. She was emotional because she faced many things in her childhood too. She wanted that in her life her partner would be the great who understands her in every way. Dia was a bright student in her school but because of this emotional breakdown she started decreasing in her studies. And one day, she got failed in her final exam and that school teachers and their class mates make a joke of her and started bulley her so badly. On that time Dia face her second rejection in a school life. Dia had a best will power she didn't give up as she stood up with the help of her god and her parents support. She started learning of her rejection and one day. And because of this emotional breakdown Dia become strong day by day and by one day Dia proved by became the CEO of the amazing company. And a best lawyer and an author of the famous book. She never gives up on her rejection she always learns something from them and become a best person. And now. Dia has married with her partner who understands her a lot and love her like no one can do. He motivated her in her this struggle and give her best wishes and faith to her. She always trusts her talent and never leave her in any situation whether it is bad or a good. Dia was lucky to have him in her life. And also, her parents proud her a lot.

"NEVER GIVE UP TO THE REJECTIONS, REJECTIONS ALWAYS GIVES YOU A CHANCE TO LEARN SOMETHING"

-SANANSHIKA MALIK

ROZY PAUL

Her name is Rozy Paul. She belongs to the tea-estate called Dibrugarh, Assam. She has done M.A. in journalism. Her hobbies are reading, gardening and cooking.

IG :writer_rozypaul

FAILURE IS OK

Take is as positive way. Its ok. Don't cry. In failure you know that success is waiting for you. So, work hard, no worries, no think of failure just work hard 24×7 work that can help you. So, success will come. If work hard result will come. If sitting and crying then failure laugh at you.so work hard and success soon reach sooner or later. There is no alternative but to work a day like a crow whole day flying in the sky to get a piece of meat and he keeps looking in the garbage, drain and big dumping place to get his food. At evening he returns every day he is searching food in gutter cleaning that is he is doing everyday so it's ok to fail working you will get success.

-ROZY PAUL (Rozy)

NAVEEN BHARDWAJ

Myself Naveen bhardwaj a programmer by profession a lover of poetry maker and like reading books and audiobooks and he has telegram channel @ThNBbook.

IG :na.vin7832

LIFE LESSON

In life I understood is everything is temporary;

In life I understood is that friendship is the only thing which will take you far in terms of relation or money;

In life I understood is that few decisions can change your life is what you choose to marry;

In life I understood rejoice your health it only thing that will keep you in shape;

In life I understood don't bother comparing yourself to other;

In life I understood accept the favourable and your reality;

In life I understood don't expect too much from other it only leads to disappointment;

In life I understood every mistake is an opportunity to learn something new;

In life I understood be happy of what you have now not what you might have been;

In life I understand experiences matters the most not what you have been through;

In life I understood you know your hidden potential but you want other permission for validation.

-NAVEEM BHARDWAJ

SRISHTI MORYA

I am SrishtiMorya. I studying Journalism. I love to write down quote, poem, story and letter to editor. My letter to editor published in a newspaper and also published poem in college magazine. I am very creative girl and an imaginary girl which create a story in dream and write in a copy. I belong to Faridabad Haryana.

IG : 4526shiny

FAILURE TEACHES THE RIGHT WAY

Failure got me whenever,

God has shown the right path,

By being together in all difficult times,

He has promoted,

Carrying hope with broken,

I have made myself more strong,

Don 't give up now let me in,

Along the right path.

Never fear defeat,

To get weaker in times,

Just taking confidence with you,

There is an advance in life.

-SRISHTI MORYA

SWAYAMSHREE CHAKRAVARTY

Co-author of 85+ anthologies, and compiler of 4 books, Swayamshree is a science student from Odisha. Besides being rude to strangers and fake smiling all the time, she's also a trained dancer and a guitarist. Influenced by her past, writing became her passion!

CANNOT BE HEALED

There are times
I want to die
Not showing my tears,
But I want to cry.
By the window when I sit
Thinking about you
I ponder, what I did wrong
To lose you.
I invested love, time
All my loyalty on us
In return I expected
Nothing more than us.
But the table was turned
Now we aren't together
No matter what, I still remember
You saying "together forever"
This line has now become a scar
Hidden for long, now revealed
All my pains can't be counted on
Leave it, it can't be healed!

-SWAYAMSHREE CHAKRAVARTY

ANKITA NAHAR

#AKII#@@@ AnkitaNahar, physically she lives in AJMER, RAJASTHAN but heartly live in everywhere. She is too much passionate about writing. She has always found comfort in words, and that's what attracts everyone. Writing is her therapy, she write what she feels and experiences in her life. You can take a look at her writings on Instagram @naharankita1.

TROUBLES AND SOLUTIONS

Troubles come and go,

Our job is how we should fight them.

The work of troubles is to bring us down,

Our job is how we should rise above them.

The work of troubles is to trouble us,

Our job is to act wisely at that time.

There is work of troubles in every work hinder,

Our job is to make them successful in any case.

The work of troubles is to make us cry every time,

Our job is to show them laughing at all times.

The work of troubles is to make us strong,

Our job is to show them by becoming strong

©AKII#@@@

-ANKITA NAHAR

ANANYA P MISHRA

She is a girl with lot of patience and as calm as sea her name is Ananya P Mishra from Bhubaneswar, Odisha. She is a student of English Honors. Believes in karma. Bookaholic. Want to set an example for this era that inspires others and me as well. Love dancing, designing and exploring new things. Self-love is priority. Always know your worth.

IG : ananya_payal191

NEVER SURRENDER-

When each and every door get closed for you,

Hope is the only thing that stands with you,

Learn to speak up for yourself

Learn to stand without anyone's else help,

Learn to say no,

Learn to face the cruel society.

Love yourself and spread that love,

Life will be hard there will be turmoils, obstacles.

Some succeed in their life,

Some failed,

Some learned from failure,

And some give up.

Giving an insight into the power of thoughts,

The effect they have on our health, body, and circumstances,

And how we become what we think.

Learn from your mistakes,

But never surrender, never give up.

-ANANYA P MISHRA (Ananya)

DEESHA SONI

DeeshaSoni..a Post Graduate and M.phil adorns the hat of a multitasker of an educationist, artist, poet ,photographer, author , blogger, homemaker, wife and mother...She has 10 years experience in the field of Education as a Professor and Coordinator. Deesha has various publications to her credit in national and international levels. Deesha has various published works to her credit... she has two books published on Amazon... named 'Just thoughts' and 'Random thoughts on pandemic'. Kindle edition and more than 100 plus published works on various online platforms of .. Deesha has been twice nominated for Author of a week award by Storymirror and has also won various recognitions in penning stories and write-ups. at National and International levels...Deesha has various published works to her credit... she has two books published on Amazon... named 'Just thoughts' and 'Random thoughts on pandemic'..Kindle edition has also won many prizes in National and international levels in many write-ups...Deesha has also published her works in 300 plus anthologies of multiple genres...

IG :deeshadauree

SHALL YOU NOT QUIT…

Shall not you quit…

Gather up courage bit by bit…

When going gets tough…

Tough gets going…

Never give up…coz you can't afford…

Be thankful you have those things others can't afford…

Never get off a flight on board…

Strive to make your own path and road…

Swim against the tides of the ocean…

Never leave when in your blood is your passion…

Don't afford to cry and sit…

Gather courage bit by bit…

-DEESHA SONI (Deesha)

BERDHISHA. P

Berdhisha is from Coimbatore, Tamil Nadu. She is pursuing her Master's degree. She is a poet who loves to share her own thoughts and imagination. Furthermore, she loves to write and read novels. She is a blogger (berdhisha96.), Co-author for about 70 Anthologies and compiling 6 Anthologies. She loves nature, which is her best friend.

IG :thoughts_of_mine_the_muse

❖I loved him wholeheartedly,

   I longed to be with him,

   he ignored me half-heartedly,

   And rejected my love,

   That makes my life as a tragic film.

❖I set a goal of my life,

   I saw failure in each of my steps

   Whatever happens I didn't give up,

   I didn't even stop climbing up,

   That shows my way to success.

❖She struggled as a baby girl,

   She struggled as an adult,

   She struggled as a woman,

   She struggled as an aged

   But she overcome everything with confidence.

-BERDHISHA .P

NILANJASHA HOWLADER

She is the NilanjashaHowlader. She is a teen of 16. She is from Kolkata, India. She is one of those beautiful blooming writers. She had worked in more than 20 anthologies as a Co-author. She is a compiler too. She is also a painter and she tries to paint her fantasies and also tries to exaggerate her thoughts on her canvas. She is also a classical singer and a dancer too. She also has huge interest in sports, she had played state–level tennis championship and she is also a boxer. She spends her leisure time in reading books and she also like to see movies. She also loves to travel and she tries to create some mind-blowing memories every time. She is a student of class 12th and currently preparing for her medical exams. She aspires to become a neurosurgeon and above all a good human being first. As a writer she believes that every human has their own way of captioning the world and she feels it is her work to capture those captions and pen them down. According to her when a writer writes, he/she not only write his /her heart out but write about a million hearts. A writer is the one who actually keep all the pains of the world in that singlesome heart. She is the one who can actually create scenes which can be related to this materialistic world.

IG : @dhur._.bhallagena

THE UNSUNG DESIRE!

It is said-
Dreams are some unfulfilled desires,
And life is too short to complete each,
Whatever I yearned for, I fail to crave for it.
Wanted to build an empire of own style!
 An Empire -
Where my voice will be sense,
Where every listener will just tune in,
To just perceive my presence!
I will be greeting a thousand "on air "
Will be trying to mingle with my glorious flares.
Inspired from some great epitomes,
Who made my childhood a treasure?
Thought to enhance it more,
By choosing it as my passion!
But not all stories end well!
My faith wasn't there in my hands,
I couldn't write my own story,
As my dreams got rejected,
In the Courts of Aspiring!
My feet got chained,
And Wings got clipped,
I couldn't complete my dreams,
I couldn't be myself,
Still regretting for it!

-NILANJASHA HOWADER

MOHAMMED NIYAZ

Mohammed Niyaz hails from Mumbai - The City Of Dreams. He often loves to write poetries and short music video stories for his own youtube channel. Apart from this Mohammed is currently working on his upcoming anthologies, as well writing poetries since 2013. You can find him on facebook/mohammedniyaz as well on

instagram @niyazsks.

❖ Flaws and mistakes are the one-off success.

   They realize you how strong you are.

   If you keep on taking a u-turn with the said tries.

   You may be the one's from the best of failures.

❖ Hard work pays you in a good sense.

   So, continue without fail to acquire your own world.

   Once you understood the concept of achievements.

   You may never lack off the way of tracks.

❖ Life has many surprises for you.

   So, accept it in all the ways it gives.

   You never know what kinda efforts you will give.

   Un till and unless you give surety for own selves.

-MOHAMMED NIYAZ (Shayar Mohammed Niyaz)

SAPNA .P

She is SAPNA PARASURAMAN born on 30.04.2003 in Pondicherry, India. A lover of Arts and Literature, a student of B.A.English Literature of BISHOP HEBER COLLEGE, TRICHY , TAMILNADU, INDIA.She is an All - Rounder person . She was also the one-day RJ of Suriyan F.M 93.5, Pondicherry. She secured 3rd place in Interschool badminton competition which was conducted by Pondicherry government. She is a good human being with humanity and helping tendencies. She likes to shine and has a selfless- mind . She is very passionate in all his works," Cool in heart, Chill in mind, makes her Character, a spicy one ". She is very ammicable and She would never put her dreams down. She is a co-author for more than fifteen books. She is also a NSS VOLUNTEER of Bishop Heber College,Trichy,Tamilnadu.

IG : sapnadeebika

EMAIL ID : sapnaparasuraman@gmail.com

INSPIRATION

A day with failure motivates to do the hardwork

A day passes with hardwork changes into frustration

A day with frustration pulls into windstorm

A day with windstorm downs your potential

A day without potential, is like a day without revolution

Finalize your life with your own motto,

One day, your motto will be your motivation

Your motivation will be your inspiration

A day you inspired others will banish

A day, you will be the inspiration to others will lavish

Move your short-term goal with inspirational people

Achieve your long-term goal with full swinging inspiration.

-SAPNA. P (Sapna Parasuraman)

NABISHBHA S.S.

Her name is Nabishbha. Currently, she is studying in the college.

❖ Success is not final, failure is not fatal.

❖ I can accept Failure, but I can't accept not trying.

❖ Failure is temporary, but it gives us permanent satisfaction.

❖ Failure is the tution, you pay for success.

❖ Ready to fail and ready to be success.

❖ We learn success only from failure, don't give up and learn not to quit.

-NABISHBHA S.S

MANSHA GOYAL

✍️She has original content 🖌️

✍️She likes to Share happiness 😇

✍️She has a GGC group

✍️ Use her #mann_ki_baate__

✍️Join her journey by tapping follow button ⬤

IG : @mnsha.writes

❖ "Mistake is secondary thing but thinking of it intentionally as you know the outcome is primary thing".

❖ "If you wanna make place in someone's heart never tell your feeling to them, because one throw is enough to break a glass".

❖ "Life is messed as puzzle pieces as it's one piece is happiness, one is problems, one is family and so on you just need to collect that piece which defines your life".

❖ "Life is a court where you are where you are witness and situation is accused".

❖ "Never mind whether a nightmare is bad or good because there always comes a brighter day".

❖ "Hope high but except less because people are always ready to pull you down".

-MANSHA GOYAL

DHANESH GHANASHYAM GAWDE

He is Dhanesh Ghanashyam Gawde 20 years guy, presently pursuing his BBI from Shri pancham khemraj college (Mumbai University), Sawantwadi, Sindhudurg, Maharashtra. He loves reading as well as writing poems, stories, etc. His hobbies are writing comics.

IG : unreliableuniform62

STRUGGLES OF OUR LIFE

Once upon a time, a daughter complained to her father that her life was miserable and that she didn't know how she was going to make it. She was tired of fighting and struggling all the time. It seemed just as one problem was solved, another one soon followed. Her father, a chef, took her to the kitchen. He filled three pots with water and placed each on a high fire. Once the three pots began to boil, he placed potatoes in one pot, eggs in the second pot and ground coffee beans in the third pot. He then let them sit and boil, without saying a word to his daughter. The daughter moaned and impatiently waited, wondering what he was doing. After twenty minutes he turned off the burners.

He took the potatoes out of the pot and placed them in a bowl. He then ladled the coffee out and placed it in a cup. Turning to her, he asked. "Daughter, what do you see?" "Potatoes, eggs and coffee," she hastily replied. "Look closer", he said, "and touch the potatoes." She did and noted that they were soft. He then asked her to take an egg and break it. After pulling off the shell, she observed the hard-boiled egg. Finally, he asked her to sip the coffee. Its rich aroma brought a smile to her face. "Father, what does this mean?" She asked. He then explained that the potatoes, the eggs and coffee beans had each faced the same adversity-the boiling water, it became soft and weak.

The egg was fragile, with the thin outer shell protecting it's liquid interior until it was put in the boiling water. The inside of the egg became hard. However, the ground coffee beans were unique. After they were exposed to the boiling water, they changed the water and created something new. "Which one are you?" He

asked his daughter. "When adversity knocks on your door, how do you respond? Are you a potato, an egg or a coffee bean?"

 Moral: - In life, things happen around us, things happen to us. But the only thing that truly matters is how you choose to react to it and what you make out of it. Life is all about leaning, adopting and converting all the struggles that we experience into somethings positive.

-DHANESH GHANASHYAM GAWDE(Unreliable)

ANISHKA NAYAK

Anishka Nayak is a dilettante writer and presently lives in Bhubaneswar, Odisha.

Writing is her hobby in leisure times and she personally believes that one can upgrade their knowledge through writing.

This is her work as co-author.

IG : @anishkanayak

FAILURES

To be successful, you have to accept all the challenges that come your way. You can't choose the challenge you like.

The number one reason people fail in life is because they listen too much to their friends, family, and neighbors.

Motivation is what gets you started. It's the habits that keep you going.

Don't be ashamed of your failure, learn from it and start again. Do what's right, in the right way, at the right time. Success comes to the one who moves quickly while he is waiting. Sometimes standing still and waiting is more valuable than moving aimlessly. Good warriors will put themselves beyond the possibility of defeat, and wait for the opportunity to defeat the enemy.

So, please don't be afraid of making mistakes

I told you before, a strategy comes from failures.

Your ability to discipline yourself to set clear goals, and then work toward them every day, will guarantee your success more than any other single factor.

Nothing of value comes easily. work, continuous work and hard work, is the only way to achieve lasting results.

-ANISHKA NAYAK

BSHI BUTT

He is a biologist, a teacher and a nature lover. He seeks chaos that is around him, and he strives for making world a better place to live in. What makes him write is the way he observes the nature and world around him. In his journey, he is hoping to cover the losses, and to get what he always dreamt of.

IG : bashibutt1

THE LOST GEM

It was an ordinary day. He was working in a mine in search of the precious stones. He kept on digging and the days passed. Days turned into months and months into years, but he didn't find that precious gem which was made for him and which could end his search for more like his destiny. His sixth sense started telling him that he was near. This thing kept him going. In the full moon night, he found a muddy stone surrounded by the dust and a lot of debris. He picked that piece and returned to home. He kept working on the piece because he thought it was the one for which he was searching. He had thought that when this piece would become gem, he would engrave it and would keep it forever. So, he did according to the plan. When he wore the ring, everyone appreciated that and dreamt to have that gem. Gem and ring both looked like they were made for each other. One day someone gave him another ring to wear. He insisted that he had his own ring, but the ring owner said no one liked to this ring. Please wear it! Please once!

So, he put his ring in pocket and wore the other one. The precious gem felt rejected by this action. The gem somehow managed to drop off from his pocket and made itself lost. When he returned to home and searched in his pocket to wear that ring again, he couldn't find it. He searched and searched everywhere but all went in vain. Alas! He lost the precious gem for which he had searched for years. Now he craves to have it back, to find it again, but sometimes life gives you only one chance and you realize it when you fail to avail it.

-BASHI BUTT (Bashi)

BIDISHA BHATTACHARYYA

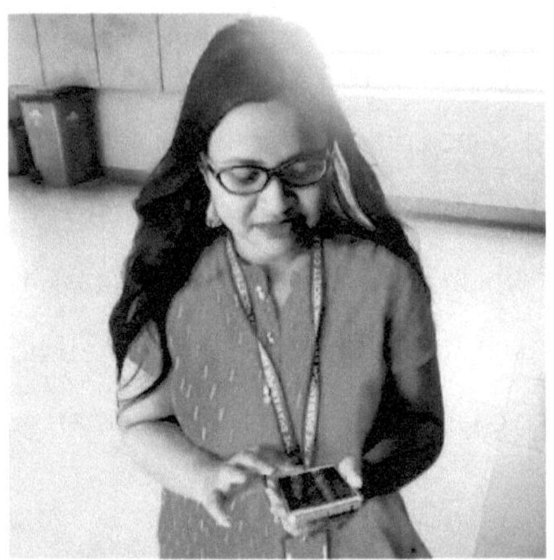

She is studying BA Honours in English Literature, 2nd year. She lives in Barrackpore, West Bengal. She has co-authored 25+ anthology books, two solo Quotebooks and one solo fiction book "Flash Pack". She has been awarded multiple times for her writing skills by companies like AwardsArc, Attainers Awards, Spectrum Awards, etc.

IG : @lovewriting1

"REJECTION IN 10 WORDS"

Hurt, failure, second chances, disappointment, mostly not meaningful, learnings, beginnings.

"SELF-LOVE LESSONS"

The best self-love lessons I have learnt are that It's okay to take breaks sometimes and take care of yourself cos your work depends on your well-being to a huge extent. You can't complete works not being physically and mentally fit.

"THE DARK"

It took a while to move forward and get out of the darkness and to bring back the light that you stole from me.

"THE GRIEF"

Grief disappears when there's consolation, happiness with hope.

-BIDISHA BHATTACHARYYA

PRACHI GUPTA

Prachi Gupta is a Passionate writer who loves to create her imaginary arts in a random canvas. She is pursuing her studies in BBA and lives in Allahabad known as the pure city of Sangam. She loves to sing and watching movies in her free time. She is a shy and an open-minded girl at the same time

For more information can follow her and contact: -

IG : @prachigupta3435

@prachi_gupta_210

EMAIL ID : Prachiguptt0210@gmail.com

JUST KEEP BELIEVING

I know, it's difficult

To move, to take further steps

But after all the storms

There is a light of hope

Where you have to believe in you

I know, so many things make you down

People insult you

Situations pull you back

But you have to keep patience for you

To get success

To keep shine after all these dark nights

I know,

There are so many hurdles, failures, toughest

circumstances in your life

But the sun shines

Even the coldest wind

To remove all the fog and enhance all the positive vibes.

-PRACHI GUPTA

NEHA KUMARI

She is Neha Kumari from Bihar. Currently pursuing Btech in Computer Science and Business System from Academy of Technology Hooghly,Kolkata .She strongly believes that if you are determined, dedicated and passionate enough you can achieve anything. There is nothing called impossible. Each and every thing is and can be made possible with the hardwork made in the right direction. She is so passionate towards writing. She has appeared in some of the anthology book as co-author and currently she is compiling a book. She believes writing our thoughts can make us feel free from worldly pressure specially when we have no one to share our problems.

IG : nkspoetry

CHOICE IS ALL YOURS!!

Life will hit you,

And will break you,

Rejections will shake you,

Not just from outside,

But also, from inside,

Wanna fly high in the sky,

Or wanna die feeling shy,

The Choice is all yours,

As this life is yours,

Decisions has to be yours,

The pain for the moment,

Or happiness for the future,

Here the decision is all yours,

The path is crystal clear,

And now if you fear,

You will cry all the years,

Now the situation is worse,

But my dear the choice is all yours.

-NEHA KUMARI

SONIYA VARGHESE

Soniya Varghese is a writer filled with her own euphoria. She is a person who remains euphoric to see the kindred and emotions evoked around her. She is an author who handles mostly romantic themes and fun thrillers which is both for teens and adults. Especially anyone who have once fallen in love in their life. Whenever she writes she takes a part from her own life. Her writings reflect all that she had experienced in her life. Anyone who reads all her writings can connect it with her life.

IG : soniya__ Varghese

FACEBOOK : Soniya Varghese

TWITTER : @SoniyaVarghese8

REJECTION IN RELATIONSHIP

Life is too short to realize who will stay with us and who will not. We all try our best to stay loyal the way we can. Even though relationships seem to have happiness outside but it's not the same when we get deep into it. And if the relationship is a little toxic one, one or the other will have to face rejections. And if one will have doubts on other than the relationship becomes too toxic.

Just talking about girls in a toxic relationship they would be rejected for everything they do. They will always have to ask permission for what they do. Like wearing clothes and make up. Still some relationship ends at break up. And these girls go back to them telling them to come back. And that's when they face the real rejection.

-SONIYA VARGHESE

PRIYA DAS

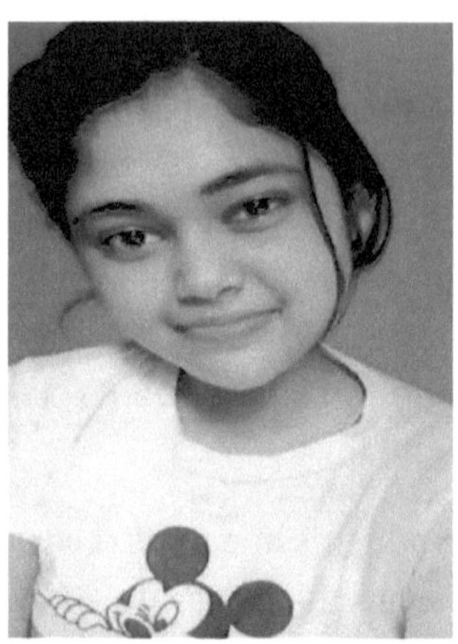

She is Priya Das belongs from a bengali family of Northeast India (Assam). She is passionate about writing and a wonderful poet. She is a trained artist, calligrapher and an amazing writer. Coauthor of 90+ anthologies. She loves to portray nature in her writings. At present she is pursuing Bsc in biotechnology. She has been winner of many daily challenges and events.

IG : @the_poet_gallery

FEARS OF FAILURES

The childhood fear is still in my heart.
The fear of failure. Though its a part of
life and no one can escape from its
 tough lesson, still the fear of getting
insulted, in the society has
dominated my mind.
We are so busy in competing with
others that we forgot to find the happiness of this beautiful
journey of life.
But, with time I learn without failure curiosity to become
better from yesterday its not possible.
 Failure is the bitter truth of our life.
People always judge us in every situation , so why to care for
them.
The failures which once hold my roots of future .
I get rid of those roots to try my best for future.
The journey of life is not meant for running away from
problems and responsibility.
Its meant to walk away from your those
things which slow downs your life race
and destroys your inner peace.
I learnt from my mistakes and
open the wings to
reach the destination.

-PRIYA DAS

SUSHRA .R

She is Sushra. She is pursuing her PG in English and supervening her dream on becoming a skillful writer. Writing always alms her with happiness. She is a strong believer of herself and exposing herself as a full-fledged person.

IG : b_l_u_l_u_v_r

MEMORIES

Me and him were friends for a long time. One day he asked me for a ride. We went to our favorite coffee shop. We entered inside. He asked me to order. As usual I ordered my favorite cappuccino. After 15 mins of his silence, he started to talk to me, we both were chatting about some crazy things and laughed at each other. Suddenly he proposed me. "I said Yes", because I loved him from the beginning. Everything went well. We made promises to stay with each other.

One day he opened our story to his parents. At first, they didn't tell anything. After a couple of days. His mother called me. She talked rudely. She said "If you don't leave my son, you are responsible for everything". I was confused and asked to her, what happened aunty? She didn't answer my question.

She just said that, "If u don't leave my son. I'll commit suicide". She ended her call. For few days, I didn't show my face to anyone. Didn't talk to anybody. Just locked myself in a dark room. "He came up to me and asked what happened?" I avoided to see him. Really, I didn't want to face him.

But, one day I called him to our favorite coffee shop. He came there. "He asked me what happened?" I replied, just leave me where it started.

Yes, I broke up with him. But still, I didn't know the reason. After that he also didn't come to me. I started to live in our memory.

-SUSHRA. R (Blueluvr)

SRIJA SADHUKHAN

Srija Sadhukhan is 19 years old girl studying BSc Biotechnology in Amity University Kolkata. Loves to write poetry and a book worm too.

IG : @syncopatemysuccess

BETRAYAL

After being disheartened by someone

My love you were a betrayer

'Coz you never tried for me.

Being in a relationship

Means both contribution

But only I tried my best on this relationship.

There is no place of lie in love

Trusting you is my decision

And proving me wrong is yours.

Why do I hate you so much now?

It's because I loved you so much

And got betrayed from you.

-SRIJA SADHUKHAN

BANDITA NAHAK

She is a young writer of 19years.She loves to write her feelings and thoughts. Her aim is to see India as a developed country. She loves to travel and explore new places.

IG : @nahakbandita

REJECTIONS – THE INJECTION FOR SUCCESS

Life is full of surprises and miracles

It's full of problems and pains

And of course, it's full of terms, conditions, rules and regulations!!

It's all about facing rejections first

And getting success after that!!

Celebrate each little rejection

It's the key to get each little success!!

Nothing is fine

I have totally lost my mind

But I have to hold on

To cross the line!

Every step I take in my life

I meet disappointment and rejections

Still there is a hope

Everything will be fine!

Because rejection is the injection for success!!

-BANDITA NAHAK

SOWNDARYA HARINI SAMPATH

Sowndarya Harini Sampath from Tirupathur District of Tamil Nadu, working as Software Engineer. She is a sports personality and an unknown artist too. Now she has started to open up minds with her writings for those who don't feel motivated and was a Co-author for thirteen anthologies and yet to go far. She was also awarded by the forever star book of world records for her fastest writings.

IG : _art_make_har_

THE BACKBENCHER

Every backbencher is always considered as an unusual stuff and believed to be an idiot who is performing always useless things other than studies and they are being rejected by the viewers or teachers/ professors from their mind with these basic thoughts. But reality is backbenchers are longing for a hand which lifts them up. One can notice every backbencher will be the real heroes/ heroines in enjoying their daily life, no matter who hurts them, they keep on enjoying and they'll be the starts of cultural and sports activities which no one knows but some will shine irrespective of the bench. Only thing they're expecting to grow is for a hand to lift them. May as the time changes, everyone will be gazing at them irrespective of the bench when they learn to lift themselves. I am writing this here as I am too was a back bencher with less grades and had more fun. Let's be happy to be a backbencher!

-SOWNDARYA HARINI SAMPATH

N. KRISHNAVENI

N. Krishnaveni is an aspiring writer and a budding poet. One of her poems "My Beloved Damsel!" has published in The Literary Herald journal. She is a co-author of many anthologies. She won the Spectrum Budding Writer Award 2021. Most of her poems deals with the theme of nature, human emotions, and philosophical thoughts. Her poetry voices out the deepest emotions and secrets that are left unspoken and destined to be beautifully inked. Having a creative artistic propaganda, her writings hails from the articulate thoughts with coherence, spontaneity and flowery language.

IG : krishi_aju

TRIUMPH BEYOND HASSLE

You are born to win

Never let your dreams die

By the trivial pains you met with

In your journey of success in disguise

Of storms and scares you like a big crisis.

In the dilemma between do or die

The choices you made at the crossroads

Won't trouble you with lament of regrets

Depends not your victory in all the games

But the choices of yours with stubborn

Of never turning to the option of quitting

As the sweetest fruit going to be ripped,

The triumph beyond hassle going to be worth.

-N. KRISHNAVENI

SMITA G NAIDU

Smita naidu is a computer post graduate with double diploma, MCA, DCA, DISM, CPISM, this is her qualification, she is working as a business head of procode technologies, which is an IT company, she is also a writer, translator, transcriber, graphic designer, entrepreneur, Youtuber, recruiter, life coach and a podcaster. As a writer, she has published more than 500. plus, quotes, which are visible on Google too, she has published a few books as coauthor too, and several are piled up, her solo book will also be published soon! She was also into forever book of world record recently, as an emerging entrepreneur.

IG : @keep_mind_and_body_healthy

WHY REJECTIONS?

Oh, I was rejected in a singing competition, while I was 5, though I gave my best,

 Oh why? Oh why?

Oh, I was rejected even when I turned ten, in an elocution competition,

 oh why? Oh why?

Oh, I was rejected when I was 12 for being the class leader,

 Oh why? Oh Why?

Oh, I was rejected for a modelling contract, when I turned 15, though I was the prettiest in the college,

 Oh why? Oh Why?

Oh, I was rejected for a job interview,

 oh why? Oh Why?

Oh, but let me tell you with all these rejections,

 I have never given up, and neither should you, take life as a game, and choose the best option, and never give up till you succeed, never pity yourself!

So, never say, why me? Why me? but instead always learn from your failures!

-SMITA G NAIDU (Simmi)

TEJASVI

Studying in the twelfth grade, he is keenly interested in infuriating the art of writing. Have a passion to pen down simple poetry in a refined way, deciphering the unravelling depictions of life, love and loss.... Though being younger in age. He still conquers the idea of inexperience and is developing his writing skills in an exceptionally admirable manner... Shares his poetry on Allpoetry (an international stage of poetry). And shares it on his Instagram blog too...!! Worked with many anthologies and as a compiler too.

IG : @dev_tejasvi_2324

TO DEFINE HER

I don't know was it our destiny
But still we met
I don't know if we'd meet again
But still I bet

I bet you'd be the only one
Deep in the core of my heart
I bet till my last breath
Death can't set us apart

You are an enchanting desire
Of the mind, the heart and the soul
You are a trigger of happiness
When your eyes are doing their role

I recall the days when we met
I witnessed you in a fabulous attire
Your cheeks and lips were mind-blowing
And your eyes - sapphires

What to tell of those moments?
Making it short I'd just say
You smiled
And all the world was gay.

-TEJASVI DEV (Tejasvi)

ANNS FETRICA J.H.

She is Anns Fetrica, currently pursuing her master degree in English literature. She is a co-author of many anthologies. She is a dream catcher and all her dreams exist in her writing. Writing moulds her into full-fledged person.

JUDGE ME?

If you say I am wrong from your point of view,

Then show me what I did that is wrong,

And you are eligible to define my mistake

Only if you are not under that category

I have my opinion in my doings,

You have your opinion in your doings,

If you find the same mistake in you,

You have no rights to reject me,

And I have many choices of my own,

I don't want you to correct me,

Either I listen to my heart beat,

If that truly hurts me then,

I go with my feelings to change me,

I am perfect of my own.

-ANNS FETRICA J.H. (Ann)

S.A. ALICE FATIMA

An emerging writer who puts her heart's longingness, desire, and rejections through words.

GLOOMING HEART

My heart glooms...

Though it's bright;

everywhere I turn, seems to be dark...

Heart aches... tears fall...

My heart aches...

Trying hard to ease myself,

watching my loved ones making fun;

am miles away from them.

First time ever,

For first time ever, I regret,

I regret for giving advice...

Voluntary advice, though valid,

is never valued...

You will be fooled...

-S.A. ALICE FATIMA

CYILRISHA A.M.

She is a simple soul who believes in the goodness of this vicious world. She loves to day-dream about stars and read books like crazy. Nothing compares to the joy she gets when she spends time with her precious friends. She strongly believes that there will come a day in everyone's life where we could live unrestrained.

IG : mag_da_leen

SO CALLED "BEAUTY"

This is not my 1st insult

In this world of adults:

'Society', is the name of that cult.

I'm nothing like the beauty they exult,

So, they lock me indoors as a result.

Men come and go, finding fault

As I was nothing like the beauty they exalt.

My mom calls me ugly by default

Saying, she has never seen such a dolt,

Indeed, because I said 'Inner beauty matters more' in revolt.

She gave a reply sharp like a bolt:

"Even if you stack millions in your bank vault

With your achievements bringing people to a halt,

A fair skin and a slimmer body matter a lot.

In your neck, to tie a knot."

So, I thought, am I a scapegoat?

-CYILRISHA A.M. (Risha)

KANCHARLA SAI SANDEEP

He is k. Sai Sandeep and he had recently completed his B.Tech in R.V.R & J.C COLLEGE OF ENGINEERING, Guntur. He is very passionate to deliver his thoughts to the fellow beings around his surroundings.

IG : sapranikk_poetry_18

THE DIVERTED MIND

We were known since childhood

Attached with a friendly bond

Helping each other to get out things easier

By reaching our goals closer

As the gap had separated us

The bonding had grown very gorgeous

That had made me fell in love with her

As she had left alone with her

Our bonding was bloomed newly

With a different name from my side

That I haven't thought it would flow continuously

That hadn't faded from her side

But her silence had a huge impact

That was beyond her act

I wish I could get her back

To get complete our love track

-KANCHARLA SAI SANDEEP (Sapranikk)